CLASS IN AMERICA

THE
ONE PERCENT

BY DUCHESS HARRIS, JD, PHD
WITH CARLA MOONEY

Essential Library

An Imprint of Abdo Publishing | abdopublishing.com

ABDOPUBLISHING.COM

Published by Abdo Publishing, a division of ABDO, PO Box 398166, Minneapolis, Minnesota 55439.
Copyright © 2019 by Abdo Consulting Group, Inc. International copyrights reserved in all countries.
No part of this book may be reproduced in any form without written permission from the publisher.
Essential Library™ is a trademark and logo of Abdo Publishing.

Printed in the United States of America, North Mankato, Minnesota
032018
092018

Cover Photo: Piti Tan/Shutterstock Images
Interior Photos: Piti Tan/Shutterstock Images, 1; Prochasson Frederic/Shutterstock Images, 5;
iStockphoto, 6–7; Red Line Editorial, 10, 94; Shutterstock Images, 12–13, 38–39, 41, 48–49, 53, 60–61,
74–75; Gino Santa Maria/Shutterstock Images, 17; North Wind Picture Archives, 19; Bettmann/Getty
Images, 20; Everett Collection/Newscom, 22–23; Everett Historical/Shutterstock Images, 25; Andy
Dean Photography/Shutterstock Images, 30; Monkey Business Images/Shutterstock Images, 33;
Polaris/Newscom, 34; Jorge Salcedo/Shutterstock Images, 42; Uladzik Kryhin/Shutterstock Images,
47; Gerry Broome/AP Images, 54; Brent N. Clarke/Invision/AP Images, 57; Andy Kropa/Invision/
AP Images, 58; Sean Locke Photography/Shutterstock Images, 65; Albin Lohr-Jones/Sipa USA/
AP Images, 66; Danny Johnston/AP Images, 69; Chutima Chaochaiya/Shutterstock Images, 70–71;
Evan Vucci/AP Images, 79; Mark Lennihan/AP Images, 82; Lynne Sladky/AP Images, 84–85; Paul
Hennessy/Alamy, 88; Lev Radin/Shutterstock Images, 91; Oleg Doroshin/Shutterstock Images, 93;
Erik McGregor/Pacific Press/Newscom, 97

Editor: Claire Vanden Branden
Series Designer: Becky Daum

LIBRARY OF CONGRESS CONTROL NUMBER: 2017961146

PUBLISHER'S CATALOGING-IN-PUBLICATION DATA

Names: Harris, Duchess, author. | Mooney, Carla, author.
Title: The one percent / by Duchess Harris and Carla Mooney.
Other titles: The 1 percent
Description: Minneapolis, Minnesota : Abdo Publishing, 2019. | Series: Class in America | Includes
        online resources and index.
Identifiers: ISBN 9781532114106 (lib.bdg.) | ISBN 9781532153938 (ebook)
Subjects: LCSH: Aristocracy (Social class)--Juvenile literature. | Economic status--Juvenile literature.
        | Distribution of wealth--Juvenile literature. | Social classes--United States--History--
        Juvenile literature.
Classification: DDC 301.451--dc23

CONTENTS

WHO ARE THE
ONE PERCENT?

I n August 2011, two New York City activists launched a Tumblr blog titled "We Are the 99 Percent." The social media site featured pictures of different people holding handwritten signs. Each explained how he or she had been affected by difficult financial times. In addition, each person identified himself or herself as part of "the 99 percent."

The 99 percent refers to the protesters' criticisms of income and wealth inequality in the United States. Feelings of anger over this inequality launched a movement known as Occupy Wall Street. The protest started in 2011 and still has influence today. In May 2011, Nobel Prize–winning economist and Columbia professor Joseph Stiglitz published "Of the 1%, by

The Occupy Wall Street movement opened the eyes of Americans to realize just how unequally wealth is distributed in the United States.

One of the most expensive mansions in the United States is located in Bel Air, California, and costs $250 million.

the 1%, for the 1%" in *Vanity Fair*. In the article, Stiglitz criticized the economic inequality in America, in which only one percent of the population owned a large portion of the country's wealth. According to Stiglitz, the top one percent of Americans earned nearly 25 percent of the country's income and controlled 40 percent of wealth. "The top 1 percent have the best houses, the best educations, the best doctors, and the best lifestyles, but there is one thing that money doesn't seem to have bought: an understanding that their fate is bound up with how the other 99 percent live. Throughout history, this is something that the top one percent eventually do learn. Too late," he wrote.[1]

"We are the 99 percent" became a powerful slogan for activists and Occupy Wall Street. They argued it was not right that one percent of the country controlled a large part of the country's wealth. They also argued that control over so much wealth gave the one percent enormous amounts of social, economic, and political power. In recent years, the idea of the "one percent" and its influence continues to be a topic of discussion. Newspaper articles, television programs, and political debates feature arguments about the effects different policies will have on the one percent as compared to the rest of America. Many people have a vague idea that the one percent refers to a few wealthy Americans. Yet when it comes down to it, many people do not have a clear idea of who it actually describes.

THE OCCUPY MOVEMENT

On September 17, 2011, several hundred people set up camps in Lower Manhattan, the heart of New York City's financial district. They marched to protest the US financial system, which they claimed favored the rich and powerful at the expense of ordinary Americans. Occupy Wall Street had begun.

The Occupy movement's message resonated with people worldwide. It sparked similar Occupy protests and camps in numerous other cities. It inspired thousands around the world to speak out against financial and social inequities. Although the protesters are no longer camped in Lower Manhattan, the Occupy Wall Street movement continues to have a lasting impact in the United States. It shone a bright spotlight on the issue of income and wealth inequality in America, bringing it into the political arena and inspiring a young generation of activists.

INCOME AND WEALTH

To understand the one percent, one must understand what the figure represents. The one percent can be defined by either income or wealth. Income is the amount of money a person receives at his or her job. Income can also be money from a business, rental income, gifts, interest or dividend income on investments, or other sources. With income, people pay for needs such as housing, food, and clothing. People also use income to pay for things they want, such as tickets to a football game or a vacation.

Another way to measure the one percent is through wealth. Wealth is the assets a person owns, such as houses, cars, stocks and bonds, savings accounts, retirement accounts, and more. Wealth is usually measured as net worth, which is total assets (houses, cars, investments, business equity, and similar things people own) minus total liabilities (mortgages, debt, student loans, and other money owed). Net worth is often measured at the household level instead of the individual level. This is because many large assets, such as a house, are jointly owned by two people. Wealth can grow over time as houses and stock investments increase in value. Wealth provides a safety net for people in case their income is disrupted. For example, if a person loses her job, she can use money in savings or an investment account to pay for living expenses until she finds another job or income source. Wealth can also be passed to future generations.

AVERAGE INCOME
OF THE ONE PERCENT
AND THE 99 PERCENT[6]

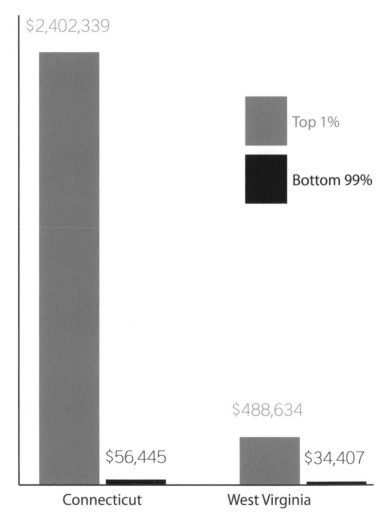

$2,402,339

Top 1%

Bottom 99%

$488,634

$56,445

$34,407

Connecticut   West Virginia

In 2013, according to a study done by the Economic Policy Institute, people in the top one percent in Connecticut had the highest average income in the country and West Virginia had the lowest.

When using income as a measure, the one percent is defined as individuals whose annual income places them in the top one percent of earners across the country. The average income of the top one percent in the United States is $1.15 million.[2] Yet, the one percent includes much more than millionaires. According to a 2016 Economic Policy Institute (EPI) report, a family with an annual income of $389,436 in 2013 fell at the bottom of the top one percent nationally. Any family with a higher income than that was part of the one percent.[3] In comparison, a family not in the one percent earned an average of $45,567 in 2013.[4] According to the EPI report, the top one percent of families earned 25.3 times as much income as the other 99 percent.[5]

When measuring income by state, the definition of the one percent can vary significantly. For example, in New Mexico,

THE WEALTHY'S WEALTH GAP

Within the one percent, another wealth gap is growing. According to a 2014 study by University of California, Berkeley, economics professor Emmanuel Saez and Gabriel Zucman, assistant professor at the London School of Economics, the top one percent can be further divided into two groups. The first group is at the bottom of the one percent. They have an average net worth of approximately $7 million, and their share of national wealth has remained about the same since 1995.[7] Those in the second group, the top 0.01 percent, have a net worth of more than $100 million, and their share of national wealth has more than doubled since 1995.[8] The top 0.01 percent are generally increasing their wealth through successful stock market investments, while the rest of the one percent are typically earning salaries.

an income of $231,276 will put a person in the top one percent. In Connecticut, however, people must earn at least $659,979 to be in the state's top one percent of earners.[9] People living in a high-wealth area such as New York or Connecticut may be technically part of the national one percent, but they may not see themselves as top earners. For example, a person in Connecticut making $400,000 may be part of the national one percent but fall far below his or her state's one-percent threshold.

THE ULTRA-WEALTHY

Often, the phrase "one percent" is an ambiguous nickname for the ultra-wealthy. The phrase evokes images of Wall Street financiers riding in chauffeur-driven limousines from their mansions to Manhattan, vacationing on yachts, and rubbing elbows with celebrities and politicians at exclusive parties. According to popular stereotypes, the one percent is willing to do just about anything to get ahead and make more money, frequently at the expense of others.

Yet in reality, the one percent is more varied than a single stereotype. The one percent includes doctors, lawyers, corporate executives, and business owners. It involves people who have inherited family money and those who have made their own. They live in communities across the United States, from New York City and Chicago, Illinois, to Denver, Colorado, and Dallas, Texas. In fact, according to the weekly financial newspaper *Barron's*, 67 percent of those in the one percent grew up in the middle class or poorer. Additionally, 76 percent "describe themselves as 'middle class' at heart."[10]

ECONOMIC INEQUALITY: A WIDE GAP

In most countries around the world, including the United States, some people have more income or wealth than others. When talking about this gap, many people focus on income inequality, or the difference in annual earnings among people. In the United States, incomes vary significantly. Americans in the top one percent earn an average of 40 times more income than those in the bottom 90 percent. The gap widens even further for those in the country's top 0.1 percent—they earn more than 198 times the income of the bottom 90 percent.[11]

While there is a huge gap in income between the one percent and the rest of the country, the divide in wealth may be even greater. According to a 2017 Federal Reserve report, the top one percent of Americans control 38.6 percent of the country's wealth, a historical high.[12] Their increase in wealth has been driven by gains in the value of assets they own and investments in the stock market. At the same time, the share of wealth owned by the bottom 90 percent of Americans continues to fall, from 33.2 percent in 1989 to 22.8 percent in 2016.[13]

When asked about the income and wealth distribution in the United States, the majority of Americans believe that income and wealth need to be more evenly distributed. In a 2015 Gallup poll, 63 percent of respondents said that wealth should be distributed more evenly. Thirty-one percent believed the current distribution was fair.[14]

DISCUSSION STARTERS

- How does being in the one percent provide an advantage to an individual?

- Why does the definition of the one percent vary by location?

- What does the term *the one percent* mean to you?

BERNIE
SANDERS

In 2016, Vermont senator Bernie Sanders made economic and income inequality one of the main themes of his campaign for the Democratic nomination in the presidential election. At a 2016 conference, Sanders spoke about the increasing gap between the rich and the poor: "In the year 2016, the top 1 percent of the people on this planet own more wealth than the bottom 99 percent [put together]. . . . At a time when so few have so much, and so many have so little, we must reject the foundations of this contemporary economy as immoral and unsustainable."[15]

Sanders's message about income inequality resonated with many Americans. After announcing his candidacy in 2015, Sanders quickly gained momentum. He drew nearly 1.5 million people to rallies and other campaign events. In the Democratic primaries, Sanders won 22 states and more than 13 million votes. His campaign drew a record 8.2 million individual contributions from donors.[16] Throughout the campaign, Sanders spoke against what he called a "rigged economy."[17] He proposed ideas such as a $15 per hour minimum wage and free public college and health care to level the economic playing field. Although Sanders eventually lost the Democratic nomination to Hillary Clinton, he became an influential force in the 2016 election.

Bernie Sanders speaking at a campaign rally in March 2016

WEALTH INEQUALITY
IN AMERICA

Unequal wealth distribution is not a new problem in the United States. Civilizations throughout history have always had some people who have more wealth and power than others. In the United States, wealth and income inequality have existed since the founding of the country. However, they were particularly pronounced in the Gilded Age.

INEQUALITY IN THE GILDED AGE

In the late 1800s and early 1900s, the United States experienced great economic growth and social change. This period of time, known as the Gilded Age, saw rapid industrialization, innovations in science and technology, the growth of cities, the construction of transcontinental railroads, and the rise

The people in the one percent in the early 1900s were considered "high society." They flourished during the Gilded Age.

of big business. The economy grew rapidly and generated enormous wealth for companies and individuals. Railroads and telephone lines stretched across the nation and created new opportunities for businesses to buy, sell, and ship goods. Industrial and financial entrepreneurs profited greatly from these

Millions of European immigrants saw America as the land of opportunity.

new business opportunities. They lived in palace-like homes and indulged in luxuries and other amusements.

During this time, wages in America were much higher than wages in Europe, particularly for skilled workers. As a result, millions of European immigrants came to America seeking higher wages and a better life for their families. However, these European industrial workers and farmers did not share in the country's new wealth. Instead, they worked long hours in dangerous conditions for low pay. As the rich grew richer, the poor struggled to survive. The gap between the country's haves and have-nots grew larger. In addition, the division of labor into unskilled and skilled careers left many workers with few marketable skills and little hope to improve their positions in life.

In the late 1800s and early 1900s, many African Americans experienced little benefit from the economic growth of the time. After the Civil War, many former slaves stayed in the South, working as laborers and sharecroppers, while some moved to the North, drawn by factory work. Most worked in low-paying, manual-labor jobs and struggled to survive day to day. In addition, African Americans faced discrimination and prejudice. This made it even more difficult for them to advance into higher-paying jobs and careers.

In 1915, a statistician named Willford I. King expressed his concern over the distribution of income in America. "If there has been an increase in the riches of the nation as a whole, has

the increase been distributed to all classes of the population, or have the benefits been monopolized by a favored few?" he wrote.[1] King calculated that approximately 15 percent of the country's income as of 1910 went to the richest one percent. Later calculations would place that number at approximately 18 percent.[2]

A NEW FEDERAL INCOME TAX

In the early 1900s, many Americans believed a national income tax was needed for several reasons. First, an income tax would provide a more stable source of income for the US government than tariffs. Also, many people believed the government's current policies allowed rich people to build too much wealth. They wanted a direct income tax to shift the burden of taxes onto the wealthy.

In 1913, the United States ratified the Sixteenth Amendment to the US Constitution. The Sixteenth Amendment gave Congress the right to impose a federal tax on incomes. Prior to 1913, the US government only collected taxes on goods, such as tariffs on imports and excise taxes on whiskey. The burden of these taxes fell on working Americans because they spent a higher percentage of their income on products that were taxed than wealthier Americans did.

Previous efforts to establish a federal income tax had been ruled unconstitutional by the courts. The main argument for the Sixteenth Amendment was that it would force the wealthy to shoulder a larger share of the federal tax burden that working Americans had largely carried in the past. A few critics of the amendment spoke out against a federal income tax. John D. Rockefeller was the founder of the Standard Oil Company and one of the richest men in America at the time. He stated, "When a man has accumulated a sum of money within the law . . . the people no longer have any right to share in the earnings resulting from the accumulation."[3]

INCOME TAX: EARLY ATTEMPTS

Although the Sixteenth Amendment established the federal income tax, it was not the government's first attempt to create a national income tax. During the Civil War, Congress passed the Revenue Tax Act of 1861. It included a tax on personal income to raise money for war expenses. The tax was repealed ten years later. In 1894, Congress again attempted to establish a national tax and enacted a flat-rate federal income tax. The US Supreme Court ruled the tax was unconstitutional.

John D. Rockefeller was once the richest man in the world. He was so wealthy that when he died, his assets accounted for 1.5 percent of the US economy at the time.

After the passage of the amendment, the first income tax law was passed in 1913. The Underwood/Simmons Tariff Act created a tax of 1 percent on incomes up to $20,000. The tax rate increased as income increased, up to 3 percent on those earning $50,000 or more. Workers did not have to pay tax on the first $3,000 earned as an individual or $4,000 as a family. Because the average worker at the time earned approximately $800 per year, most did not have to pay any federal income tax. In fact, less than 4 percent of American families earned more than $3,000 annually.[4] In the first year, the government collected $71 million in income taxes. John D. Rockefeller paid an estimated $2 million. At the time, many people believed that the income tax was a good idea.

GREAT DEPRESSION REDUCES INEQUALITY

Despite the new income tax, income inequality continued to rise into the 1920s. By 1928, the wealthiest one percent of Americans earned 23.9 percent of all income. The bottom 90 percent earned

INCOME TAX TODAY

More than a century after the ratification of the Sixteenth Amendment, income tax in America has changed significantly. The original 15-page tax code has expanded to more than 1,000 pages of complex rules and formulas. Most Americans did not pay any federal income tax in 1913 because they did not meet the income threshold. Today, however, approximately 56 percent of Americans pay federal individual income tax.[9] Even those who do not pay federal individual income taxes still pay other taxes, such as state income taxes, sales taxes, and property taxes. In 2015, the federal government collected $1.54 trillion from individual income taxes, making it the federal government's largest source of revenue.[10] Some critics of today's complicated tax system have called for the country to move to a simpler flat tax. This is an income tax system in which everyone pays the same tax rate regardless of income. Others want to get rid of federal income taxes entirely and replace them with a national sales tax.

only 50.7 percent.[5] In 1929, the stock market crashed and wiped out wealth for millions of investors. The crash triggered the Great Depression, the worst economic downturn in America's history. For several years, consumer spending and investment dropped. This led to steep declines in industrial production. Failing companies laid off workers. By 1933, nearly 15 million Americans were unemployed. Nearly half of the country's banks had failed, causing millions to lose their savings.[6]

The Great Depression dramatically reduced income inequality. By 1944, the top one percent's share of income was approximately 11.3 percent. The bottom 90 percent received 67.5 percent.[7] For the next three decades, these levels would remain mostly constant.

After World War II (1939–1945), the United States entered a period of economic growth and shared prosperity. According to economics professor Robert H. Frank, incomes in the United States rose rapidly at approximately 3 percent a year for people at all income levels.[8] More Americans considered themselves part of a vibrant middle class. Roads and bridges were well maintained. New infrastructure was built around the country. Shared prosperity helped people of all incomes improve their lives and fortunes. Most of these benefits, however, were for white men. Minorities and women were often excluded from equal opportunities in the workforce.

THE PROGRESSIVE MOVEMENT

During the late 1800s and early 1900s, the United States experienced tremendous change. The country began to shift from an agricultural society of farmers to a more industrialized one where people lived in cities and worked in factories. The shift brought about many social changes. Millions of workers relied on businesses and factory owners for their jobs and wages. Sometimes, the business owners did not pay workers a fair wage and forced them to work long hours in dangerous conditions. Many people also believed that wealthy business owners had unfair influence over the government.

In the 1890s, a group known as Progressives called for reform. Often college-educated, middle-class Americans, Progressives believed that while industrialization was good for society, it caused many problems. They wanted employers to treat workers fairly, with better pay, safer working conditions, shorter hours, and increased benefits. They also believed strongly in education and fought for child labor laws that would keep children out of mines and factories and in schools. The Progressive movement is credited with spearheading many reforms to reduce the gap between the rich and poor in the early 1900s. They included increased wages, regulation of massive corporations, and the passage of a federal income tax.

INEQUALITY RISES AGAIN

The economic growth and shared prosperity enjoyed by Americans began to change in the mid to late 1970s. The country entered a decade of slow economic growth, high unemployment, and high inflation. New government policies such as deregulation of business and tax changes attempted to stimulate the economy.

At the same time, the income share of the top one percent began to rise significantly, while the bottom 90 percent's share began to fall. The share of total income collected by the top

10 percent of households increased from 34.6 percent in 1980 to 48.2 percent in 2008.[11] Much of this increase was driven by the share of total income collected by people in the top one percent. Their share of income rose from 10 percent in 1980 to 21 percent in 2008.[12] The incomes of the top 0.1 percent of households also rose sharply during this period, making the United States one of the world's most unequal countries.

THE GREAT RECESSION

In 2007 and 2008, the Great Recession affected households across the United States. A few years before the Great Recession, housing prices rose quickly as people invested in real estate. Eventually, these inflated prices were unsustainable and housing prices fell quickly. When these inflated housing prices plummeted, it triggered a financial crisis. Consumer spending and business investment slowed significantly, and businesses laid off many employees. The Great Recession hit many people hard. Average Americans lost jobs and investments. In 2008 and 2009, the United States lost 8.4 million jobs, which was 6.1 percent of all payroll employment.[13] It was the largest reduction in employment of any recession in the country since the Great Depression. Investments in homes became worth little. Some people even found themselves owing more on their homes than they were now worth. Even the one percent felt the pinch of the recession. Significant declines in the stock market and in house and property values caused the wealth of the one

More than three million houses were foreclosed during 2008 due to the Great Recession.

percent to drop dramatically. Because of the significant losses for the one percent, the divide between the one percent and the rest of the country narrowed.

While the Great Recession reduced income inequality, its effect was only temporary. Many middle-class and lower-income families struggled to recover. In the three years following the recession, the average American family's income decreased 5 percent and its wealth dropped 2 percent. The average family did not add to retirement savings and took on more student debt. During this period, the only households that experienced income gains were the highest earners. This again increased the gap between the one percent and the rest of the country. The stock market surged and property values rebounded, allowing the wealthy to recover much faster. Today, the gap between the wealthiest one percent and the rest of the country continues to grow.

DISCUSSION STARTERS

- Why did the Great Depression lessen income and wealth inequality in America?

- Do you think the federal income tax has worked to reduce income inequality? Why or why not?

- Compare the recovery from the Great Recession for the one percent and the other 99 percent. How did they differ? What caused this difference?

THREE

WHAT CAUSES
INCOME AND WEALTH
INEQUALITY?

I n a capitalist society, no one expects everyone to have the same amount of income and wealth. It is natural for income to vary among people with different skills, experience, and education levels. A person who has 30 years of experience in a job can reasonably expect to earn a higher income than a worker who recently graduated from college. In the same way, older Americans often have more wealth than younger Americans, simply because they have had more years to save and invest money. Yet since the 1970s, the gap between the one percent and the rest of the country has steadily widened. There is no easy answer as to why this has occurred. But economic experts believe that several factors have played a role in income and wealth inequality in America.

Capitalism is a system in which private companies buy or sell goods for a profit.

Technology is even starting to take the place of delivery drivers. Amazon is developing a delivery service known as Prime Air, which uses drones to drop off packages right on people's doorsteps.

TECHNOLOGICAL CHANGE

Since the 1970s, advances in technology have changed lives around the world. Because of technology, people are able to talk on cell phones, shop on the internet, and work on a laptop from any location. Technology has also changed the way companies do business. New technologies, automation, and computers have made a variety of tasks, from bookkeeping to designing new products, faster and more efficient. Many of these technological advances have benefited those in the one percent. They can afford to purchase the latest cell phones, laptop computers, and other technologies. With these devices, the one percent can be more efficient and effective, both at work and at home.

In the United States, automated technology allows businesses and factories to complete the same tasks with fewer human workers. Many blue-collar jobs that paid well in the past have been eliminated and replaced with technology. Most of these jobs were filled with people in the 99 percent. With fewer jobs available, these displaced workers have had to turn to jobs in other industries, such as retail or other services that do not pay as well. At the same time, there have been more opportunities for engineers and other highly skilled employees, positions that are often filled by people in the one percent. This has benefited people in the one percent. The country is offering more jobs in these high-paying fields, and employers in the one percent don't need to hire as many workers to get a job done. With companies paying top dollar for these skilled employees, the income gap between skilled and unskilled workers is growing. Workers with at least a bachelor's degree can earn approximately $1 million more in their working lifetime than less-skilled workers with only a high school diploma.[1] This is according to a 2014 report from the Federal Reserve Bank of New York.

Erik Brynjolfsson is a professor at the MIT Sloan School of Management. He argues that advances in computer technology, including robots, automation, and software, have been a major factor in the slow employment growth of recent years. Along with fellow researcher Andrew McAfee, Brynjolfsson tracked productivity and total employment in the United States. In the years after World War II, the two metrics moved closely together. Increases in jobs matched corresponding increases in productivity. As businesses helped workers become more productive, everyone benefited. The increase in productivity drove economic activity and created more jobs. Beginning in 2000, this relationship began to change. Brynjolfsson found that while productivity continued to rise, employment stopped growing. By 2011, a significant gap appeared between the two measures. While the country experienced economic growth, there was no related increase in jobs. Brynjolfsson believes that technology explains the change. "It's the great paradox of our era," he said. "Productivity is at record levels, innovation has never been faster, and yet at the same time, we have a falling

THE WORKER WAGE GAP

Technology advances have affected both skilled and unskilled workers, reducing the number of jobs available. Unskilled workers are often hit harder by technology. As technology replaces human workers, companies still need skilled workers to use computers and operate high-tech equipment. The increased demand for these skilled workers increases wages for these jobs, while wages for the remaining unskilled jobs remain flat or even drop. As a result, the income gap between skilled and unskilled workers widens.

DECLINE OF THE LABOR UNION

Since 1983, membership in labor unions in the United States has fallen by almost half. A labor union is an organized group of workers, often in a similar trade or profession, that forms to protect the workers' rights and interests. Labor unions typically negotiate wages, benefits, and working conditions with company owners on the workers' behalf. In 2014, 11 percent of US workers were union members, according to the US Bureau of Labor Statistics.[3] Some people believe that the decline in union membership has also been a factor in rising inequality. This is due to the fact that union wages are typically higher than nonunion wages. In some cases, when companies pay lower wages and benefits to workers, stockholders and company owners can benefit from greater company profits.

median income and we have fewer jobs. People are falling behind because technology is advancing so fast and our skills and organizations aren't keeping up."[2] According to Brynjolfsson, technology is the biggest factor in the recent increases in inequality.

OUTSOURCING

However, technology has also brought the world closer than at any other time in history. People and companies can easily communicate, trade, travel, and do business with people on the other side of the globe. At the same time, American workers and companies face more competition than ever from abroad.

Changing global trade has been difficult for some industries. Many developing countries have lower worker costs than industrialized nations, which gives them a cost advantage when

Many US companies have expanded to Asia. The larger consumer base is extremely lucrative for those in the one percent.

producing manufactured goods. As a result, some US companies moved their manufacturing facilities to developing countries to take advantage of lower wage costs. This process is known as outsourcing. Doing so allowed the companies to compete more effectively in the global marketplace and improve their net earnings. This then benefits stockholders and company owners, which directly benefits those in the one percent.

GLOBAL SUPERSTARS

While technological change and globalization are driving down workers' incomes and reducing the number of jobs available in the United States, other factors are increasing the income of the one percent. These advances have made it easier for the most talented people to capture a larger share of

the market or charge higher prices for their services. To examine this phenomenon, consider the case of a person diagnosed with cancer. The patient wants to find the best medical care possible. Before communication and transportation advances, the person would seek the services of the best doctor in his or her city. Today, the patient can have a videoconference over the internet with doctors in distant locations. With enough money, the patient can fly anywhere in the world to consult with the best doctors on the planet. Doctors with the best reputations quickly find their demand has skyrocketed. Because their services are in high demand, professionals can charge much higher prices than other doctors providing comparable services.

The idea of the superstar exists in many industries, from medicine and engineering to business and finance. Because companies are no longer limited to a specific geographic area to find talent, they can search the world for the most highly skilled executives and employees. The demand for top skills is another factor in rising inequality. As companies pay more to hire and retain top employees, certain individuals reap huge rewards. These individuals fall in the one percent.

EDUCATION

Since the early 1980s, the value of a college degree has increased more quickly than that of a high school diploma. In 2015, young adults (ages 25 to 34) working full-time with at least a bachelor's degree earned an average of $50,000 annually according to the

Thanks to technology, people can have consultations with the best doctors from around the world.

National Center for Education Statistics. Those with only a high school diploma earned $30,500.[4] The expertise and skill that are demonstrated by earning a college degree can lead to greater income and economic rewards.

Even for people who earn a college degree, there are large differences in lifetime earnings depending on a person's area of study. While income growth slowed or even stopped for many workers in the 2000s, people with science, technology,

engineering, mathematics, and business skills and education often experienced good salary growth, even in the midst of the Great Recession. For example, from 2000 to 2014, workers in computing fields saw their wages increase approximately 6 percent.[5] Business, finance, and engineering workers also experienced similar gains. People who have these degrees are more likely to be in the one percent. At the same time, people with degrees in some liberal arts fields, such as sales and teaching, saw their incomes decline. This, among other factors, leads to the widening gap between those in the 99 percent and those in the one percent.

THE COLLEGE PREMIUM

The college premium is the increase in income that workers with a college degree earn compared to workers without a degree. From 1980 to 2005, the college premium doubled as the demand for workers with a college degree was greater than the supply. Some economists estimate this gap in income was responsible for approximately 60 percent of the increase in wage inequality between 1973 and 2005.[6]

TAX POLICIES

Some economists believe that changes in the US tax policy since the 1970s have also contributed to the rising income inequality in America. Since the end of World War II, the top individual federal tax rates have declined significantly. A marginal tax rate is the tax rate a person pays on his or her next dollar of income. In a progressive tax system, people pay increasing tax rates as their incomes rise. For example, using 2017 federal tax rates, a person pays 10 percent on the first $9,325 of income and 15 percent tax on income dollars between $9,325 and $37,950. If he or she earns any more income, it would be taxed at the next higher tax rate of 25 percent. This is the person's marginal tax rate.[7] In 1945, the top marginal tax rate was 94 percent. In the 1970s, it dropped to 70 percent. By the mid-1980s, the top rate had dropped to 50 percent. By 2003, it was 35 percent. Although the top rate in 2017 has risen slightly to 39.6 percent, it is still much less than tax rates half a century ago.[8] As a result, the federal tax code has become much less progressive, which means tax rates increase more slowly when taxable income rises. Those in the one percent are paying less in taxes than they were 70 years ago. Therefore, they get to keep a higher percentage of their money.

Other changes in tax policy have also played a role in rising wealth inequality. Under the current tax code, people pay a far lower tax rate on capital gains and other investment income than they do on regular wages. This tax policy benefits the wealthy, who are more likely to have large gains and income

CAPITAL GAINS TAX

Capital gains tax is a federal tax on certain types of investments or properties that a person sells for a profit. A capital gain is an increase in the value of an investment or real estate that a person holds. Capital gains income is not recognized until a person sells the asset. For example, if a person buys a share of stock at $100 and sells it at $150, he has a capital gains income of $50. He will owe capital gains tax on the $50 profit.

from investments. According to a study by the Congressional Research Service, reductions in the federal tax rate for capital gains income is one of the largest contributors to rising income inequality.

There is no one clear cause for the rising wealth inequality in the United States in recent years. Instead, a multitude of factors have combined and had an impact on wealth at the top and bottom of the income scale. Changes in technology, globalization, education, tax rates, and the increasing demand for high skills are all part of the widening gap between the one percent and the rest of the country.

DISCUSSION STARTERS

- Why do you think the choice of major in college affects a person's future income and wealth? What educational choices can people make to preserve their incomes and wealth?

- How do you think workers should adapt to technological advances to preserve their incomes and wealth?

- What impact do you think globalization and outsourcing has had on the one percent?

FOUR

EFFECTS OF WEALTH
INEQUALITY

S ome economists argue that a certain level of inequality
is necessary because it motivates people to grow the
economy and be innovative. Yet others believe the
wealth gap can have a negative impact on society. They warn
that if the gap grows too wide and more wealth is concentrated
in fewer hands, inequality can have ripple effects across the
country. It can negatively impact economic growth, politics,
education, and even health and life span for all.

IMPACT ON ECONOMIC GROWTH

According to American economist Arthur Okun, society cannot
have both perfect equality and perfect efficiency. Instead, a
society must choose how to best balance the two. Without the

Silicon Valley in northern California is a famous
technology hub. It also holds the second-highest
concentration of wealthy people in the United
States (after Connecticut).

The spending habits of the middle class have a huge impact on the economy.

promise of a large financial reward, entrepreneurs, inventors, and other innovators would have less incentive to develop new products, processes, and other innovations that drive economic growth.

While some economic inequality motivates people to work hard and innovate, the growing inequality gap may have a negative effect on the country's economic growth. Research shows middle-class Americans often spend a larger percentage of their incomes than the wealthy. As middle-class incomes decline, spending also drops, which slows the economy's growth. "Our middle class is too weak to support the consumer spending that has historically driven our economic growth," wrote Stiglitz.[1] "With inequality at its highest level since before the Depression, a robust recovery will be difficult in the short term, and the American dream—a good life in exchange for hard work—is slowly dying."[2]

HEALTH

People in the one percent have the advantages of wealth in regards to their health. They can afford to pay for top health insurance packages, top doctors and hospitals, and state-of-the-art treatments and therapies. They can afford to take time off work to recover from illness. On the other hand, people who have less money may find their health suffers because they do not have access to these resources. They may put off seeing a

CRIME

Some studies of income and wealth inequality have found the widening gap between the one percent and the rest of the country may have a negative effect on American society. First, some researchers have found a relationship between income inequality and crime. According to a review of research conducted between 1968 and 2000, researchers say there is evidence that economically unequal societies have higher crime rates.[3] Some researchers suggest that one reason this may occur is because lower-income people may be resentful or hostile because of their economic position. This may make them more likely to commit crimes. Additionally, economic inequality increases the incentive to commit crimes. Some people may decide that the benefits of gaining assets through crime are greater than the risk of getting caught and punished. In addition, law enforcement may spend more efforts and money to reduce crime in the affluent neighborhoods of the one percent. This leaves a less effective police force in less wealthy areas, which can lead to a higher rate of crime.

doctor or getting treatment because they cannot afford to pay or cannot take time off work to go.

Income inequality may even negatively affect the health of everyone in a community, including the one percent. A 2015 study from researchers at the University of Wisconsin Population Health Institute looked at several risk factors that affected the health of people in various counties in the United States. In their results, they found that people living in communities with higher income inequality were more likely to die before age 75 than people living in communities with more equal income distribution. This occurred even if the average income of the communities was the same. In places with more economic inequality in a community, more residents died before age 75.[4]

Scientists are working to better understand the reason for this drop in life expectancy. One theory is that having money makes a bigger difference for people on the low end of the income ladder than those at the top. When incomes are more equal, there are fewer very poor people in a community, and also fewer very rich people. The boost to health from having fewer poor is greater than the negative effect of fewer rich. Then, overall, the community's average health and life span increases. Another theory involves the dynamics of the community itself. Some researchers suggest that economic inequality causes more tension in American society. This can lead to more stress, fear, and insecurity for everyone, all of which can negatively affect health.

EDUCATIONAL OPPORTUNITIES

The growing economic gap between the one percent and the rest of the country can also affect a person's educational opportunities. Children from high-income families are more likely to do better in school and have more educational opportunities than children from lower-income families. According to a 2012 report by Sean Reardon, a professor of education and sociology at Stanford University, the achievement gap between children in high-income and low-income families has widened as the income gap between the two groups also widened. The achievement gap grew by 40 percent between 1976 and 2001.[5]

The achievement differences begin at an early age. Children coming from families in the one percent do better in school than those in the lower 99 percent. Those in the one percent are able to afford enrichment opportunities, such as tutors, music, and art, which increase their knowledge from an early age.

SEGREGATED BY INCOME

In recent years, residential segregation by income has increased significantly. High-income families buy homes in expensive neighborhoods where less well-off families cannot afford to live. This segregation by income reduces the interaction between the poor and the rich throughout the community.

Many privileged kids attend private school, a luxury that many in the 99 percent can't afford.

School quality is also a factor in the achievement gap among children from different income backgrounds. Today's public schools are mainly funded by real estate taxes in the communities they serve. Neighborhoods with expensive homes and high-income residents have more funding and offer more opportunities to students. As a result, schools in higher-income neighborhoods often have state-of-the-art facilities and experienced teachers.

Many celebrities donate to the presidential candidates they support. Rock musician Bon Jovi supported Hillary Clinton in 2016.

POLITICAL INEQUALITY

The rising concentration of wealth can make inequality more difficult to correct, as those in the one percent use their money and influence to sway politicians to maintain policies that preserve their wealth. Studies have shown that the rich are more politically involved than others. In a 2014 study, researchers from Northwestern University interviewed 83 members of the one percent about their political activities. They compared the responses from those people to responses from the rest of the country collected in a 2009 Pew Research Center survey. Across several political activities, those in the one percent were the most engaged. "By several measures, wealthy Americans participate politically at two or three times the rate of members of the general public as a whole," wrote the researchers.[6] In the 2008 election, 99 percent of the wealthy said they had voted, compared to a 70 percent voter turnout rate for lower-income Americans.[7] In addition, the wealthy were "three times more likely to talk about politics, four times more likely to attend a political event, and six times more likely to donate to political campaigns compared to Americans in the lowest income group," according to the *Washington Post*.[8]

In the United States, candidates for a variety of political positions need private funding in order to be effective. Successful candidates for Congress often spend millions of dollars on their election campaigns, buying advertisements, holding rallies, and distributing information. While spending money does not guarantee that a candidate will win, studies have found that there is a correlation between campaign spending and votes. To raise money for their campaigns, candidates often court wealthy donors. After they are elected, officials are hesitant to support policies that are not favored by their wealthy donors because they might lose their financial support.

DISCUSSION STARTERS

- Why do you think some people support policies that may increase economic inequality?

- Do you think having wealth influences the political process? Explain your answer.

- What do you think we can do to reduce the achievement gap in schools?

FIVE

RACE AND
ETHNICITY

S ince its beginnings, the United States has been a melting
pot for people from around the world. People from
Europe, Asia, South and Central America, and Africa have
come to live in America. In recent decades, the United States has
become even more racially and ethnically diverse. According
to a report from the US Census Bureau, all racial and ethnic
groups other than whites grew faster than whites from 2015
to 2016. "While all other groups experienced natural increase
(having more births than deaths) between 2015 and 2016," the
Bureau said, "the non-Hispanic white alone group experienced a
natural decrease of 163,300 nationally."[1] Non-Hispanic whites still

As of January 2018, the vast majority of the
wealthiest people were white men. Amazon
founder Jeff Bezos then had more than
$70 billion.

remained the largest group at 198 million, however, followed by Hispanics at 57.5 million and African Americans at 46.8 million.[2]

While the country is becoming more racially and ethnically diverse, it is also becoming more divided by wealth and income. According to a 2011 report by news website theGrio, black households accounted for only 1.4 percent of the top one percent by income, while white households made up nearly 96.2 percent of the top one percent by income.[3]

WEALTH GAPS ALONG RACIAL AND ETHNIC LINES

According to recent research, the wealth gap between whites and minorities in the United States is significant. In 2015, Demos and the Institute on Assets and Social Policy released a study on the racial wealth gap. They reported that the median white household had $111,146 in wealth in 2011. In contrast, the median African American household had only $7,113 in wealth—just 6 percent of the figure for whites. Hispanic Americans did not fare much better, holding a median $8,348 in wealth, approximately 8 percent of the figure for whites.[4]

According to the report's authors, today's wealth gap along racial lines can have a significant effect on inequality in the future and affect who reaches the one percent. While not every household will become wealthy, every family needs a certain amount of wealth for security. Because households of color

have less wealth today, African American and Hispanic young adults are much less likely than their white peers to receive money from family members to invest in their futures. Therefore, they have fewer opportunities than white people to enter the one percent. The researchers suggest the racial wealth gap is being driven by three main factors: homeownership, education, and labor markets.

HOMEOWNERSHIP

For most Americans, their home is their largest asset, the biggest piece in their wealth portfolio. "Homeownership is the central vehicle Americans use to store wealth, so homeownership and access to homeownership are at the heart of that widening wealth gap," said Catherine Ruetschlin, senior policy analyst for Demos.[5] Because homeownership is such an important part of wealth, it is also a critical piece on the path to the one percent. Yet in the United States, homeownership is not equal by race and ethnicity. Hispanics and African Americans are less likely than whites to own a home, and when they do, the homes are often worth less. According to a 2015 study by Demos and the Institute on Assets and Social Policy, 73 percent of white families own their homes, while only 47 percent of Hispanics and 45 percent of African Americans are homeowners.[6] For those who own a home, the amount of equity or money they have invested in the home also varies. The typical home equity for white homeowners was $86,800 as compared to $48,000 for Hispanic homeowners and $50,000 for African American homeowners.[7]

One reason race affects homeownership and home values is because people from white households are more likely to receive inheritances or other assistance from family members. This helps them fund an initial down payment on a house. With this help, they can purchase

IMMIGRATION POLICY

For people not born in the United States, immigration policy is another barrier to better jobs and moving into the one percent. The United States has several laws that protect the rights of all employees, regardless of immigration status. However, immigrant workers often face barriers enforcing these protections. Because many are not familiar with the US labor market, they may be more likely to stay in jobs they are familiar with, even if the job pays less and has fewer benefits. These factors prevent them from moving up the career ladder and joining the one percent.

a home earlier than many African American and Hispanic home buyers, who must wait longer to build up the down payment needed to buy a house. This early start gives white home buyers an advantage and head start in building equity in the home. This, in turn, increases their wealth and their likelihood of becoming part of the one percent.

Many factors influence the homeownership rates of African Americans and Hispanics. In the past, federal housing policies discriminated against blacks. For example, the National Housing Act of 1934 denied services to entire African American neighborhoods in a practice known as redlining. Redlining is denying services directly or indirectly to residents of certain areas based on the racial or ethnic makeup of those areas. Redlining discouraged banks from lending to people living in these areas and made it more difficult for them to buy homes. Even though the practice of redlining was banned in 1968, its impact still exists as white families received a head

WELLS FARGO ADMITS DISCRIMINATION

In 2012, Wells Fargo Bank, the largest residential home mortgage originator in the United States, admitted that it had engaged in discrimination against qualified African American and Hispanic borrowers from 2004 through 2009.[8] The bank steered qualified minority borrowers toward high-interest loans while giving white borrowers with similar credit more-favorable terms. In addition, the bank charged approximately 30,000 African American and Hispanic borrowers higher fees and rates than white borrowers because of their race or national origin. In a settlement with the Department of Justice, the bank agreed to pay $184.3 million in compensation to affected borrowers.

start in creating wealth through homeownership. Blacks and Hispanics are more likely to live in areas with lower home values and higher poverty rates as compared to neighborhoods where the residents are mostly white. In addition, people of color face discriminatory lending practices. Banks often charge people of color higher interest rates on mortgages, even among borrowers with the same credit scores, which makes borrowing for a mortgage more expensive.

In addition, the Great Recession of 2007 and 2008 hit many black and Hispanic households harder than white households. In the housing crash and Great Recession, the median white family lost 16 percent of its wealth. In comparison, the median African American family lost 53 percent and Hispanic families lost 66 percent.[9] For households that could no longer make their mortgage payments, foreclosures on the home destroyed any wealth or equity they had built up in the home.

EDUCATION

More students than ever are enrolling in four-year colleges. Earning a college degree is an increasingly important factor in a person's ability to earn a good income, build wealth, and have a chance to become part of the one percent. However, even as more students are going to college, including African American and Hispanic students, the barriers to earning a degree have contributed to the gap between white students and students of color in recent years. In 2011, 34 percent of white students completed a four-year college degree, while only 20 percent of African Americans and 13 percent of Hispanics completed a degree.[10]

Even if they earn a college degree, students of color may still be starting behind white students. Often, students of color graduate college with higher debt levels than white students, which affects their ability to build wealth. More of their income is used to pay back student debt instead of saved. In addition, discrimination in the workplace may make it more difficult for people of color to obtain higher-paying jobs. These factors put students of color behind in building wealth and make it more difficult for them to reach the one percent.

Hispanics have significantly less student loan debt than African Americans or white people. This is partly because Hispanics who do attend college typically go to community college, which is cheaper than a four-year degree.

In 2016, Ford Foundation president Darren Walker announced the Inclusive Growth of Cities Campaign. The program works with other groups and city mayors around the world to create programs that reduce inequality.

LABOR MARKET

Differences in the labor market also contribute to the racial wealth gap and who is part of the one percent. For most Americans, the majority of income comes from a paycheck. In addition, employers often provide workers with subsidized health insurance, paid leave, and retirement plans. Employees who have access to these benefits are better able to build wealth and are more likely to be part of the one percent. For example, the higher a person's income, the more money she can save and invest. If an employer provides or pays for a portion of health insurance, employees have to spend less of their own money to buy insurance. In addition, some employers offer retirement plans like 401(k)s and pensions that give employees an easy way to save and invest, building wealth. These plans often have an employer contribution, an amount of money the employer contributes to the employee's retirement account, which further helps the employee build wealth.

Working for employers in jobs that provide these important benefits gives a person an advantage in building wealth. However, workers of color often work in jobs that pay less and have fewer benefits. While the typical white family makes about $50,400 annually, African American and Hispanic families make only $32,038 and $36,840 respectively.[11] In addition, African Americans and Hispanics are less likely to have jobs that include benefits that those in the one percent enjoy, such as health insurance, retirement plans, or paid leave. With these benefits, those in the one percent don't need to use their current income to pay for health expenses. This gives them much more of an opportunity to save and build wealth. In the same way, African American workers also have higher rates of unemployment, which drains their savings and reduces their ability to build wealth. These are issues those in the one percent don't have to worry about.

DISCUSSION STARTERS

- What barriers to homeownership do people of color face?

- What factors have contributed to the wealth gap between Americans of color and white Americans?

- Have you ever experienced or witnessed barriers for working people because of race or ethnicity? What happened?

SIX

THE GENDER
WEALTH GAP

ccording to the 2010 US census, 50.8 percent of Americans are female.[1] Despite accounting for slightly more than half the population, women are not equally represented in the top one percent. According to a 2014 paper by researchers at the National Bureau of Economic Research, the gap between women and men in the top one percent, while decreasing, is still fairly large. Of the earnings of all people in the top one percent, women earned only 11 percent of the total.[2] "The glass ceiling is still there, but it is thinner than it was three decades ago," wrote the paper's authors.[3]

In 2018, the richest woman in the United States was Alice Walton, heiress of Walmart. Her net worth was estimated then at $47.4 billion.

One solution to help more women enter the one percent is to get them into science, technology, engineering, and math (STEM) fields.

GENDER PAY GAP

On June 10, 1963, President John F. Kennedy signed the Equal Pay Act into law. The law said that men and women were to receive equal pay for "substantially equal" work for the same employer. The following year, the US Congress passed the Civil Rights Act of 1964. This act provided protections against discrimination based on gender, national origin, race, and religion.

Yet despite this legislation, women in the United States are still often paid substantially less than men. According to a 2016 report by the US Congress's Joint Economic Committee, a woman working full-time, year-round, typically earns only 79 cents for every dollar earned by a male coworker.[4] This means that a woman working the same job as a man earns less than four dollars for every five dollars he earns.

This difference is known as the gender pay gap, and it adds up over time. Over one year, this means a woman earns $10,800 less than a man, based on median annual earnings. Over an entire career, the gender pay gap can add up to nearly half a million dollars.[5] Since the 1960s and 1970s, when women first began entering the labor market in large numbers, the gender pay gap has decreased significantly. However, it still exists in many industries and is not projected to close until 2059.[6] As a result, women are less likely to reach the one percent than men.

Even when women do reach the top one percent of incomes, they are less likely to stay there. In the early 1980s, a top-earning woman who reached the one percent was in danger of falling back through the so-called "paper floor" and slipping back into a lower-earnings income bracket within one year.[7] In 1981,

THE PAY GAP AND RETIREMENT INCOME

The gender pay gap has a significant effect on women's retirement income. This occurs because the most common sources of income for a retired person are Social Security benefits, pensions, earnings, and personal savings. These sources are generally based on a person's work and earnings history. For women who earn less than their male coworkers over a career, the retirement income is also less. In 2014, the median annual income of women aged 65 and older was $17,400, an amount that is only 56 percent of men's income at the same age.[8] In addition, women are more likely than men to postpone retirement, according to a survey by the National Institute on Retirement Security. Women reported several reasons for postponing retirement, including making up for lower career earnings.

64 percent of women in the top 0.1 percent and 74 percent in the next 0.9 percent would fall into a lower income bracket within a year. In comparison, only 43 percent of men in the top one percent would drop into a lower income bracket.[9] However, times might be changing. A 2014 study by the National Bureau of Economic Research suggests that women who reach the top one percent are much more likely now to stay there and are as likely as men to remain.[10]

MANY FACTORS

Economists believe that many factors play a role in the gender pay gap and contribute to the lack of representation for women in the one percent. One factor is the lack of family-friendly workplaces for many Americans. Many families are unable to find affordable, quality child care and are not offered paid family leave by their employers. When one parent has to take time off a job or reduce hours to care for children, women are significantly more likely to do so. As a result, millions of working women are forced to choose between their careers and their families. Women who are in the one percent have the money to hire help, such as a nanny, to help take care of the children, a luxury that most in the 99 percent cannot afford.

Among parents of young children, mothers are more likely to stop working to care for children than fathers. When children are under the age of three, 56 percent of mothers work outside the home as compared to nearly 90 percent of fathers.[11] Even for

those who do work outside the home, more mothers report having to take a significant amount of time off work to care for a child or other family member. Twenty-seven percent report having to quit their jobs in order to care for children and family members. In contrast, only 10 percent of fathers reported that they quit their jobs because of family responsibilities.[12]

Taking a career time-out or reducing work hours has a significant effect on a woman's career path and lifetime earnings and makes it more difficult for her to become part of the one percent. For example, if a woman who earns an annual salary of $30,000 stays home with her children for five years, she loses more than $150,000 in earnings. In addition, she also gives up the raises, contributions to retirement plans and Social Security, and promotions she could have

earned had she continued working. Over that same time, her male coworkers continue to earn salaries and receive bonuses, raises, and other benefits—especially men in the one percent.

"Many women are forced to sacrifice their career to care for their family. This reality depresses women's earnings, contributing to gender pay inequality," wrote the authors of the 2016 Joint Economic Committee report.[13]

GENDER AND RACE

For women of color, the gender pay gap is even larger. On average, African American women earn only 60 cents and Hispanic women earn 55 cents for each dollar earned by a white man.[16] Over a lifelong career, this gap is significant. A typical African American woman would earn $877,000 less than a typical white man over 40 years. For Hispanic women, the gap is even greater. They would earn over $1,000,000 less than a typical white man.[17]

GENDER WEALTH GAP

Over time, the pay inequality between men and women also causes a gender wealth gap and makes it more difficult for women to accumulate enough wealth to be part of the one percent. According to a 2015 report, single women have only 32 cents saved for every dollar of wealth owned by a man.[14] "The wealth gap is a much more meaningful gap both in terms of overall economic stability and how well women are able to provide for their own future and their family's future," said Mariko Chang, a former sociology professor at Harvard University.[15]

Some researchers have found that there are some differences in the savings behaviors of men and women. A 2015 survey by the investment company BlackRock found that women were more risk averse in savings and investing than men. Those in the one percent are more likely to take on a high-risk investment than those in the 99 percent. In addition, many women, even high earners, were reluctant to take an active role in managing their money and savings. These differences in behaviors are an explanation for why some women fall behind their male peers in building wealth and are less likely to be part of the one percent.

DISCUSSION STARTERS

- What is the difference between the glass ceiling and the paper floor? How does each contribute to women's ability to reach the one percent and remain there?

- Do you think women today are still encouraged to pursue lesser-paying careers, or has that changed in your experience?

- Can you think of any other factors that might contribute to the gender pay gap and women's ability to reach the one percent?

SEVEN

WHAT SHOULD
BE DONE?

M any people agree that something must be done about the widening wealth gap, both globally and in the United States. However, there is less agreement about how exactly to reduce wealth inequality. While some call for more taxes on the one percent, others argue that social policies to improve education and generate good-paying jobs will be more effective in reducing wealth inequality in the long term.

ROLE OF THE GOVERNMENT

A majority of Americans believe the government should have a leading role in reducing wealth inequality. In a 2013 *Washington Post*–ABC News poll, 57 percent of respondents said they believed the government should pursue policies to reduce

President Trump signed a new tax law in December 2017 that aimed to take less money out of each middle-class paycheck. Critics said the law will only help the rich get richer.

the wealth gap between wealthy and less-well-off Americans.[1] Nearly two out of three respondents said current federal policies benefited the rich over average Americans.[2]

However, even those who support more government involvement to reduce wealth inequality admit that it might not make a lot of difference. Claudia Goldin is the Henry Lee Professor of Economics at Harvard University. She believes economic forces that maintain unequal wages and unequal wealth will not disappear because of new government laws and policies. "I think it is naïve of most individuals to think that for everything there is something that government can legislate and regulate and impose that makes life better for everybody," she said. "That's just not the case."[3]

MAKE TAXES MORE PROGRESSIVE

To reduce income inequality, some people suggest that tax rates for the one percent should be raised to redistribute wealth from that group to the rest of the country. Currently, the United States' tax code is progressive, which means that people who make the most money pay the highest tax rates, while the poor pay the lowest rates. However, there are many loopholes that those in the one percent can take advantage of to reduce their tax burdens.

In particular, capital gains, which are profits from the sale of property or investments, and dividend income from investments are currently taxed less than regular income. People in the one percent are more likely to have accumulated wealth in property and investments. They benefit when income generated from the sale of these assets is taxed at a lower rate. Some economists believe that adjusting capital gains tax rates to make them similar to income tax rates can help reduce wealth inequality.

The estate tax is another area where tax reform could help reduce wealth inequality. Members of the one percent often pass along their wealth to their children upon their death. An estate tax is a tax on the transfer of any assets or liabilities from a deceased person to his or her heirs. Increasing estate taxes could limit the amount of wealth the one percent passes down through families.

However, critics of tax reform argue that this will do little to solve the problem of wealth inequality. A study from the Brookings Institution found that increasing taxes on the wealthy and increasing transfers to the poor would have little effect on inequality. The study looked at what would happen if the top income tax rate was raised from 39.6 percent to 50 percent and additional tax revenue was redistributed to households in the lowest 20 percent of incomes. The researchers assumed that

The New York Stock Exchange, which is located on the famous Wall Street, is where stocks are bought, sold, and traded. Selling stocks is one way to earn capital gains.

there would be no change in behavior from the top earners to reduce their income and as a result reduce their taxes. The additional tax revenue of $96 billion amounted to a transfer of

$2,650 to each lower-income household, a small amount that would not have a significant effect on wealth inequality.[5] "That such a sizable increase in the top personal income tax rate leads to a strikingly limited reduction in income inequality speaks to the limitations of this particular approach to addressing the broader challenge," wrote the report's authors.[6]

Some argue that economic growth depends on people who are ambitious, driven, and skilled risk-takers. Therefore, the United States needs people to be constantly reaching for more in order to power economic growth. And to motivate them, they must be rewarded for their efforts, skills, and risks. Although these rewards lead to inequality, some argue that this might not be such a bad thing. According to economist Gary Becker, "It would be hard to motivate the vast majority of individuals to exert much effort, including creative effort, if everyone had the same earnings, status, prestige, and other types of rewards."[7]

LUXURY TAX BACKFIRES

In 1991, Congress imposed a luxury tax on items purchased by the rich, such as high-priced cars, private aircraft, jewelry, furs, and yachts. The tax worked to reduce the number of frivolous, luxury items the rich bought. However, it also had unintended consequences on the economy. The wealthy's drop in luxury purchases had a ripple effect across several industries. Businesses in the jewelry, aircraft, and boating industries faced smaller sales and revenues, which caused them to cut back staff. Thousands of Americans working in these industries lost their jobs. Eventually, the luxury tax was repealed.

Protesters in Miami fight in 2015 for a higher minimum wage, which would help more people enter the middle class.

RAISING LOW INCOMES

Other people argue that the best way to reduce economic inequality is to help people on the lower end of the income and wealth scale improve their situations. Some policies to reduce wealth inequality focus on raising low incomes.

One popular proposal is to raise the minimum wage. In 2017, the federal minimum wage was $7.25 per hour. Many people believe that raising the minimum wage to $10.10 or higher would help lower-income workers make ends meet and save more, which would allow them to start building wealth. Raising the minimum wage to $10.10 would lift 4.6 million people out of poverty, according to researchers from the University of California, Berkeley.[8] Yet, critics argue that while a higher minimum wage would raise many

low-wage workers above the poverty line, it would do little to address income and wealth inequality.

ENCOURAGE SAVINGS

Policies that encourage savings and lower the cost of building assets for low-income and middle-class households can help the 99 percent build wealth. According to the nonprofit Corporation for Enterprise Development (now known as Prosperity Now), 140 million Americans have no or very little savings.[9] Without savings, they have nothing to use as an emergency cushion for unexpected expenses such as hospital bills or car repairs. Unlike those in the one percent, they live paycheck to paycheck, without building wealth for the future.

EIGHT MEN

The eight richest men in the world own as much wealth as half of the world's poorest population, approximately 3.6 billion people, according to a 2017 report by Oxfam International, a confederation of charitable organizations focused on reducing global poverty.[10] "It is obscene for so much wealth to be held in the hands of so few when 1 in 10 people survive on less than $2 a day. Inequality is trapping hundreds of millions in poverty; it is fracturing our societies and undermining democracy," said Winnie Byanyima, executive director of Oxfam International.[11] "Across the world, people are being left behind. Their wages are stagnating yet corporate bosses take home million dollar bonuses; their health and education services are cut while corporations and the super-rich dodge their taxes; their voices are ignored as governments sing to the tune of big business and a wealthy elite."[12]

To help more Americans save, policies can establish programs that automatically enroll workers in retirement plans and savings plans that make it easier for them to save and build wealth. Programs that provide a savings credit or a federal match for worker contributions to a retirement plan can also help workers build wealth. In addition, policies to create fair, low-cost access to financial services and homeownership are also ways to encourage savings and build wealth.

INVEST IN EDUCATION

A quality, affordable education is one of the most powerful ways to fight wealth inequality. "Good education empowers Americans to move up the economic ladder. But today the education system fails millions of low-income students and is no longer the great opportunity equalizer. So it is time to take some sorely needed actions to shake things up," said Stuart M. Butler, a senior fellow in economic studies at the Brookings Institution.[13] Investments in education, beginning with early-childhood programs, can improve education across the country. Other suggestions to improve K–12 education include longer school days and hours, small-group tutoring, and higher expectations of students.

Access to affordable education is also critical. "Sixty-five percent of jobs by 2025 will require some sort of post-secondary education. So we need to invest more in accessing post-secondary education and encouraging young people in particular," said Monique Rizer.[14] She serves as executive director

Bill and Melinda Gates have used their money and status as people in the one percent to create the Bill and Melinda Gates Foundation, which invests in many different causes, including education.

of Opportunity Nation, a bipartisan organization working to close opportunity gaps in America. The rising cost of colleges and universities in America is a barrier to reducing income and wealth inequality. As the cost of college keeps increasing, many students are taking out more loans to pay for it. As a result, they ate with a larger burden of student debt, which strangles their ability to save and start building wealth. Some economic experts suggest changing the federal financial aid system to increase the amount of money students can receive in grants. These do not have to be paid back, which could make college more affordable for low-income students.

DISCUSSION STARTERS

- How much should the government be involved in efforts to reduce wealth inequality? Explain your position.

- What do you think is the best solution to the problem of wealth inequality?

- What are the pros and cons of tax redistribution policies to reduce the wealth gap?

EIGHT

THE FUTURE OF THE
ONE PERCENT

T he gap between the one percent and the rest of the United States is projected to keep rising at least until 2035, according to a report from the Congressional Budget Office.[1] By that time, it will have steadily widened for nearly 60 years.

TECHNOLOGY'S FUTURE IMPACT

Technological advances in communications, computing, and automation have greatly changed the world and the way people live and work. In the future, advances in areas such as robotics and artificial intelligence may widen the gap between the haves and the have-nots even more. Workers in almost every industry will be at risk of seeing their incomes drop or even losing their jobs to automation. Companies "have discovered that robotics,

The economic future of the one percent is closely tied to the rise and fall of the stock market.

machine learning and artificial intelligence can replace humans and improve accuracy, productivity and efficiency of operations," says Darrell West, the founding director of the Center for Technology Innovation at the Brookings Institution.[2] At the same time, automation that reduces company costs may lead to more money for owners and stockholders.

For example, Amazon employs tens of thousands of warehouse workers. The company has begun using robots in its warehouses and is testing how they can grab products from a shelf and put them into a tub. Some people believe that as robotic technology improves, the number of robots in Amazon's warehouses will increase at the expense of the company's human workers.

Experts predict that workers in almost all industries, from telemarketers to data-entry specialists, are at risk of their jobs becoming computerized and automated in the future. At the same time, new technologies will be a huge benefit for others.

ECONOMIC MOBILITY

Economic mobility is the core of the American dream. It is the ability of a person to move up and down the income ladder. According to a study by the Pew Charitable Trusts, more than 40 percent of Americans believe that hard work, ambition, and drive are the most important factors to propel a person up the economic ladder.[3] Although there may be inequality in the United States, economic mobility gives individuals the hope that they will be able to work hard and rise to a new income and wealth level.

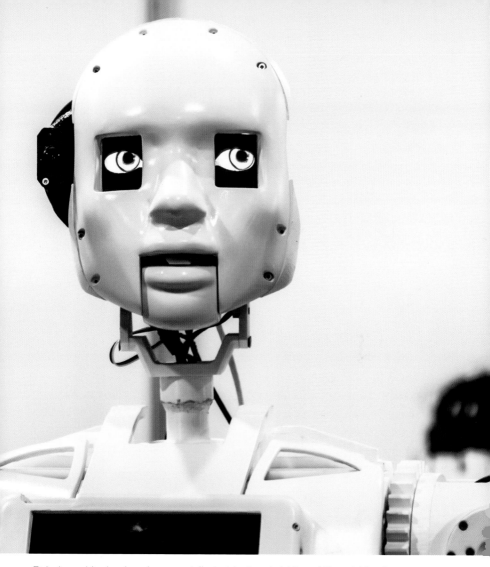

Robots and technology have contributed to the shrinking of the middle class and the growth of the one percent in America.

"There's never been a better time to be a worker with special skills or the right education because these people can use technology to create and capture value," wrote economists Erik Brynjolfsson and Andrew McAfee.[4] Owners and stockholders in tech companies will also benefit. Experts warn that if the issue is not addressed, the gap between rich and poor will grow.

SHIFTING CLASSES

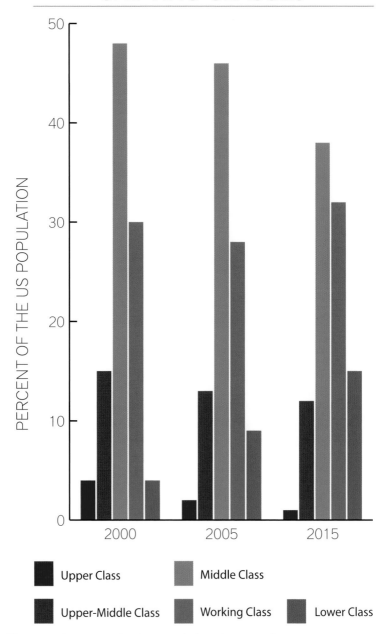

These are the trends of social class in America according to a survey done by Gallup. The middle class is shrinking while the lower class is growing. The upper class has shrunk since 2000 as well.

A GROWING THREAT

Some experts predict that if the growing gap between the one percent and the 99 percent is not reigned in, the deepening divide will threaten the US and global economies. According to a 2017 report released by the World Economic Forum (WEF), the increasing gap between the rich and poor has become one of the biggest threats to the global economy.[5] Increasing wealth inequality has triggered a wave of protests against free trade and global economic connections in the United States and other countries. The WEF warns that globalization could slow and even reverse unless countries take action to reduce wealth inequality.

Rising wealth inequality may even become serious enough to threaten democracy in the United States and in countries worldwide. More people have started to feel that the political system and government rules are rigged to favor the rich, leaving them frustrated and with few options to improve their own lives. Many are angry and no longer believe that the government can deliver results for the average person.

A PROBLEM EXAGGERATED?

While some people view rising wealth inequality as a serious threat, others are not so sure. They point out the gap between the rich and the poor decreases significantly after considering the wealth redistribution programs already taking place, such as taxes and social welfare programs. While inequality is not entirely eliminated by these programs, they argue that it may not be as big of a problem as portrayed.

In addition, critics argue whether wealth inequality should be considered a problem at all. In a 2016 Cato Institute Policy Analysis paper, the authors argue that most rich people earned their wealth by providing goods and services that benefited the country as a whole. Also, they argue there is still a good amount of economic mobility in the United States. They state that a person who is rich today may not be rich tomorrow, while a person who is poor today may be able to climb out of poverty tomorrow. "Although we are frequently told that we are living in a new Gilded Age, the US economic system is already highly redistributive. Tax policy and social welfare spending substantially reduce inequality in America. But even if inequality were growing as fast as critics claim, it would not necessarily be a problem," said Michael Tanner, a Cato Institute senior fellow.[6]

A SIDE OF FRIES?

One day in the not-so-distant future, people may order hamburgers and fries from a machine. The Bureau of Labor Statistics estimates that 80,000 fast-food jobs will disappear by 2024 as workers are replaced with machines.[7] Fast-food jobs are considered some of the most likely to be automated in the future. Companies will find it cheaper and more efficient to buy a robotic arm to serve customers than to hire a human employee.

INEQUALITY VS. UNFAIRNESS

While much of the focus on economic inequality has centered on the gap between the rich and poor, some researchers argue that many people actually prefer unequal societies. In a 2017 paper, researchers from Yale University report that humans actually prefer living in a world with inequality. They explain that if everyone is equal, studies suggest, many people become angry or bitter if their hard work is not rewarded or if those who do not work hard receive the same rewards. "We argue that the public perception of wealth inequality itself being aversive to most people is incorrect, and that instead, what people are truly concerned about is unfairness," said Christina Starmans, one of the Yale researchers who worked on the paper.[8]

Therefore, instead of focusing on an income or wealth gap, the existence of unfairness may be a better definition of

MILLENNIALS NOT WORRIED

While many Americans worry about robots taking over their jobs, millennials have embraced technology. In a 2017 World Economic Forum survey, nearly 80 percent of young people aged 18 to 35 years said they believed technology was creating, not destroying, jobs for humans.[9] As a whole, the group was optimistic about the impact of technology on their future jobs. They talked about artificial intelligence and robotics as some of the most promising technology trends. Respondents also indicated that the education, health-care, and manufacturing sectors would likely benefit the most from new technological advances in the future.

the inequality problem. When unfairness exists, some people receive preferential treatment, while others are treated unjustly. "In the present-day United States, and much of the world, these two issues are confounded, because there is so much inequality that the assumption is that it *must* be unfair. But this has led to an incorrect focus on wealth inequality itself as the problem that needs addressing, rather than the more central issue of fairness," said Starmans.[10]

Wealth inequality has become a pressing issue in America today. The riches of the one percent compared to the needs of the 99 percent are debated in living rooms, offices, and political forums across the country. By examining and understanding the causes and effects of inequality, Americans may be better able to reduce unfairness and poverty for all citizens.

DISCUSSION STARTERS

- How do you think we can use technological advances to reduce income inequality instead of increasing it?

- Can a society have income inequality and still be fair?

- Do you believe the problem of wealth inequality in America has been exaggerated? Why or why not?

ESSENTIAL FACTS

SIGNIFICANT EVENTS

- In 1913, the first national income tax was established, which was permitted by the Sixteenth Amendment to the US Constitution.

- In 1929, the stock market crashed and triggered the Great Depression, the worst economic downturn in America's history. The Depression wiped out the wealth of many and dramatically reduced income inequality.

- After decades of shared prosperity, income inequality rose again in the 1970s.

- In 2007, the housing bubble burst and triggered the Great Recession. While the wealthy quickly rebounded from the financial crisis, middle-class families struggled to regain income and wealth.

- In 2011, protesters marched as part of the Occupy Wall Street movement to protest income inequality and the US financial system, which they claimed favored the rich and powerful at the expense of ordinary Americans.

KEY PLAYERS

- Vermont senator Bernie Sanders made economic and income inequality one of the main themes of his campaign for the Democratic nomination in the 2016 presidential election.

- Nobel Prize–winning economist and Columbia professor Joseph Stiglitz has studied wealth inequality in the United States and criticized the fact that only one percent of the population owns a large portion of the country's wealth.

IMPACT ON SOCIETY

In most countries, including the United States, some people have more income or wealth than others. In the United States, the income and wealth gap between the top earners (the one percent) and the rest of the country continues to grow. Left unchecked, this divide between the one percent and the remaining 99 percent can affect everyone. Economic inequality can negatively impact the country's economic growth, health, and educational opportunities. The concentration of wealth into the hands of a few can also impact the political process, giving too much influence to the wealthy.

In recent years, many people have begun to stand up and speak out to reduce the wealth gap between the one percent and the rest of the country. Although there are some wealth redistribution efforts in progress, such as taxes and social welfare programs, there is still a lot more work to be done. By understanding how economic inequality appears in society and the effect it can have on people across the country, people can make changes to bring about a more equal and inclusive economic system for all people.

QUOTE

"The top 1 percent have the best houses, the best educations, the best doctors, and the best lifestyles, but there is one thing that money doesn't seem to have bought: an understanding that their fate is bound up with how the other 99 percent live. Throughout history, this is something that the top one percent eventually do learn. Too late."

— *Economist Joseph Stiglitz, May 2011*

GLOSSARY

ACHIEVEMENT GAP
Any significant and persistent difference in academic performance or educational attainment between different groups of students by race, ethnicity, or economic status.

ACTIVIST
A person who campaigns to bring about political or social change.

CAMPAIGN
A planned series of activities designed to produce a particular result such as a political or social goal.

CAPITALISM
An economic system in which businesses are privately owned and operated for the purpose of making a profit.

DISCRIMINATION
Unfair treatment of other people, usually because of race, age, or gender.

DIVIDEND
A regular payment made by a company or other entity, divided among many people.

ETHNICITY
A group that has a common national or cultural tradition.

EXCISE TAX
A tax charged on the purchase of a specific product.

FORECLOSURE
The action of taking possession of a mortgaged property after the person who borrowed money can no longer make mortgage payments.

GLOBALIZATION
The movement toward a world more connected by trade, finance, and communications.

INCOME INEQUALITY
The unequal or uneven distribution of income among households or individuals.

INTEREST
A fee charged when a person or business borrows money.

LABOR MARKET
The supply and demand for labor.

PROGRESSIVE TAX
A tax in which the tax rate increases as the taxable amount increases.

RECESSION
A period of negative economic growth and, usually, low demand for goods and high unemployment.

RISK AVERSE
Wanting to make an investment with the least amount of risk.

TARIFF
A set of prices, fees, duties, or taxes on imported or exported goods.

ADDITIONAL
RESOURCES

SELECTED BIBLIOGRAPHY

Barrett, Jennifer. "What's Worse Than the Gender Wage Gap? The Wealth Gap."
CNBC.com. CNBC, 3 Sept. 2015. Web. 19 Jan. 2018.

Pazzanese, Christina. "The Costs of Inequality: Increasingly, It's the Rich and the
Rest." *Harvard Gazette*. Harvard University, 8 Feb. 2016. Web. 19 Jan. 2018.

Porter, Eduardo. "Education Gap Between Rich and Poor Is Growing Wider."
New York Times. New York Times Company, 22 Sept. 2015. Web. 19 Jan. 2018.

Stiglitz, Joseph E. *The Great Divide: Unequal Societies and What We Can Do about
Them*. New York: Norton, 2015. Print.

Traub, Amy, and Catherine Ruetschlin. "The Racial Wealth Gap: Why Policy
Matters." *Demos.org*. Demos, 21 June 2016. Web. 19 Jan. 2018.

FURTHER READINGS

Bair, Sheila. *The Bullies of Wall Street: This is How Greed Messed Up Our Economy*.
New York: Simon, 2016. Print.

Harris, Duchess, and Laura K. Murray. *Class and Race*. Minneapolis: Abdo,
2019. Print.

ONLINE RESOURCES

To learn more about the one percent, visit **abdobooklinks.com**. These
links are routinely monitored and updated to provide the most current
information available.

MORE INFORMATION

For more information on this subject, contact or visit the
following organizations:

CENTER FOR ECONOMIC AND POLICY RESEARCH
1611 Connecticut Ave. NW, Suite 400
Washington, DC 20009
202-293-5380
cepr.net

The Center for Economic and Policy Research is a national research
organization working to promote democratic debate on the most important
economic and social issues that affect people's lives.

ECONOMIC POLICY INSTITUTE
1225 Eye St. NW, Suite 600
Washington, DC 20005
202-775-8810
epi.org

The Economic Policy Institute is a nonprofit, nonpartisan think tank created
in 1986 to include the needs of low- and middle-income workers in economic
policy discussions.

WASHINGTON CENTER FOR EQUITABLE GROWTH
1500 K St. NW, Eighth Floor
Washington, DC 20005
202-545-6002
equitablegrowth.org

The Washington Center for Equitable Growth is a national research
organization founded to accelerate cutting-edge analysis into whether and
how structural changes in the US economy, particularly related to economic
inequality, affect growth.

SOURCE NOTES

CHAPTER 1. WHO ARE THE ONE PERCENT?

1. Joseph E. Stiglitz. "Of the 1%, By the 1%, For the 1%." *Vanity Fair.* Condé Nast, May 2011. Web. 7 Feb. 2018.

2. Kathleen Elkins. "Here's How Much You Have to Earn to Be in the Top 1% in Every US State." *CNBC.* CNBC, 12 June 2017. Web. 7 Feb. 2018.

3. Estelle Sommeiller, Mark Price, and Ellis Wazeter. "Income Inequality in the US by State, Metropolitan Area, and County." *EPI.* Economic Policy Institute. 16 June 2016. Web. 7 Feb. 2018.

4. Elkins. "Here's How Much You Have to Earn to be in the Top 1% in Every US State."

5. Sommeiller, Price, and Wazeter. "Income Inequality in the US by State, Metropolitan Area, and County."

6. Sommeiller, Price, and Wazeter. "Income Inequality in the US by State, Metropolitan Area, and County."

7. Robert Frank. "The Other Wealth Gap—the 1% vs. the 0.01%." *CNBC.* CNBC, 31 Mar. 2014. Web. 7 Feb. 2018.

8. Frank, "The Other Wealth Gap—the 1% vs. the 0.01%."

9. Elkins. "Here's How Much You Have to Earn to be in the Top 1% in Every US State."

10. Richard C. Morais. "Who Are the One Percent?" *Barron's.* Dow & Jones Company, Inc., 6 May 2012. Web. 1 Feb. 2018.

11. "Income Inequality." *Inequality.org.* Institute for Policy Studies, n.d. Web. 1 Feb. 2018.

12. Robert Frank. "The Top 1% of Americans Now Control 38% of the Wealth." *CNBC.* CNBC, 27 Sept. 2017. Web. 7 Feb. 2018.

13. Frank, "The Top 1% of Americans Now Control 38% of the Wealth."

14. Frank Newport. "Americans Continue to Say US Wealth Distribution is Unfair." *Gallup.* Gallup News, 4 May 2015. Web. 7 Feb. 2018.

15. David Usborne. "Bernie Sanders Tells Vatican Conference Income Inequality Worse Than a Century Ago." *Independent.* Independent Co., 15 Apr. 2016. Web. 8 Feb. 2018.

16. Frank, "The Top 1% of Americans Now Control 38% of the Wealth."

17. Bernie Sanders. "A Rigged Economy." *Bernie Sanders.* Friends of Bernie Sanders, 8 Nov. 2015. Web. 7 Feb. 2018.

CHAPTER 2. WEALTH INEQUALITY IN AMERICA

1. Timothy Noah. *The Great Divergence: America's Inequality Crisis and What We Can Do About It.* New York: Bloomsbury, 2012. 10.

2. Noah, *The Great Divergence,* 10.

3. "The Income Tax Amendment: Most Thought It Was a Great Idea in 1913." *CRF-USA.* Constitutional Rights Foundation, n.d. Web. 8 Feb. 2018.

4. "The Income Tax Amendment."

5. Drew Desilver. "US Income Inequality, on Rise for Decades, Is Now Highest since 1928." *Pew Research.* Pew Research Center, 5 Dec. 2013. Web. 7 Feb. 2018.

6. "Great Depression." *History.* A&E Television Networks, LLC, n.d. Web. 7 Feb. 2018.

7. Desilver. "US Income Inequality, on Rise for Decades, Is Now Highest since 1928."

8. Robert Frank. "Income Inequality: Too Big to Ignore." *New York Times.* New York Times Company, 16 Oct. 2010. Web. 7 Feb. 2018.

9. Roberton C. Williams. "A Closer Look at Those Who Pay No Income or Payroll Taxes." *Tax Policy Center*. Brookings Institution, 11 July 2016. Web. 7 Feb. 2018.

10. Drew Desilver. "High-Income Americans Pay Most Income Taxes, but Enough to be 'Fair'?" *Pew Research*. Pew Research Center, 13 Apr. 2016. Web. 7 Feb. 2018.

11. Desilver. "US Income Inequality, on Rise for Decades, Is Now Highest since 1928."

12. Carolyn B. Maloney and Charles E. Schumer. "Income Inequality and the Great Recession." *JEC Senate*. United States Congress Joint Economic Committee, Sept. 2010. Web. 7 Feb. 2018.

13. "The Great Recession." *The State of Working America*. Economic Policy Institute, n.d. Web. 7 Feb. 2018.

CHAPTER 3. WHAT CAUSES INCOME AND WEALTH INEQUALITY?

1. Jaison R. Abel and Richard Deitz. "Do the Benefits of College Still Outweigh the Costs?" *New York Fed*. Federal Reserve Bank of New York, 2014. Web. 8 Feb. 2018.

2. David Rotman. "How Technology Is Destroying Jobs." *Technology Review*. MIT Technology Review, 12 June 2013. Web. 8 Feb. 2018.

3. "Union Members—2014." *BLS*. Bureau of Labor Statistics US Department of Labor, 23 Jan. 2015. Web. 8 Feb. 2018.

4. "Annual Earnings of Young Adults." *NCES*. National Center for Educational Statistics, Apr. 2017. Web. 8 Feb. 2018.

5. Jonathan Rothwell. "Is Income Inequality Really Unrelated to Education?" *Brookings*. The Brookings Institution, 3 Mar. 2015. Web. 8 Feb. 2018.

6. Timothy Noah. *The Great Divergence: America's Inequality Crisis and What We Can Do About It*. New York: Bloomsbury, 2013. Print.

7. "Federal Tax Brackets." *Money Chimp*. Money Chimp, n.d. Web. 8 Feb. 2018.

8. "US Federal Individual Income Tax Rates History, 1862–2013 (Nominal and Inflation-Adjusted Brackets)." *Tax Foundation*. Tax Foundation, 17 Oct. 2013. Web. 8 Feb. 2018.

CHAPTER 4. EFFECTS OF WEALTH INEQUALITY

1. Steve Hargreaves. "How Income Inequality Hurts America," *CNN*. Cable News Network, 25 Sept. 2013. Web. 8 Feb. 2018.

2. Hargreaves, "How Income Inequality Hurts America."

3. Nicholas Birdsong. "The Consequences of Economic Inequality." *Seven Pillars Institute*. Seven Pillars Institute, 5 Feb. 2015. Web. 8 Feb. 2018.

4. Margot Sanger-Katz. "Income Inequality: It's Also Bad for Your Health." *New York Times*. New York Times Company, 30 Mar. 2015. Web. 8 Feb. 2018.

5. Sean F. Reardon. "The Widening Academic Achievement Gap Between the Rich and the Poor." *FRBSF*. Federal Reserve Bank of San Francisco, 2012. Web. 8 Feb. 2018.

6. Christopher Ingraham. "The 1 Percent Is Way More Politically Active Than You Are." *Washington Post*. Washington Post, 30 Sept. 2014. Web. 8 Feb. 2018.

7. Ingraham, "The 1 Percent Is Way More Politically Active Than You Are."

8. Ingraham, "The 1 Percent Is Way More Politically Active Than You Are."

CHAPTER 5. RACE AND ETHNICITY

1. Bill Chappell. "Census Finds a More Diverse America, as Whites Lag Growth." *NPR*. National Public Radio, 22 June 2017. Web. 8 Feb. 2018.

2. Chappell. "Census Finds a More Diverse America, as Whites Lag Growth."

3. "Who Are the Black '1 Percent'?" *TheGrio*. TheGrio, 21 Nov. 2011. Web. 8 Feb. 2018.

SOURCE NOTES
CONTINUED

4. Laura Sullivan, Tatjana Meschede, Lars Dietrich, and Thomas Shapiro. "The Racial Wealth Gap." *Demos*. Demos, 2015, Web. 8 Feb. 2018.

5. Laura Shin. "The Racial Wealth Gap: Why a Typical White Household Has 16 Times the Wealth of a Black One." *Forbes*. Forbes, 26 Mar. 2015. Web. 8 Feb. 2018.

6. Sullivan, Meschede, Dietrich, Shapiro, "The Racial Wealth Gap."

7. Sullivan, Meschede, Dietrich, Shapiro, "The Racial Wealth Gap."

8. "Justice Department Researches Settlement with Wells Fargo Resulting in More Than $175 Million in Relief for Homeowners to Resolve Fair Lending Claims." *Justice*. United States Department of Justice, 12 July 2012. Web. 8 Feb. 2018.

9. Rakesh Kochhar, Richard Fry, and Paul Taylor. "Wealth Gaps Rise to Record Highs between Whites, Blacks, Hispanics." *Pew Social Trends*. Pew Research Center, 26 July 2011. Web. 8 Feb. 2018.

10. Shin, "The Racial Wealth Gap: Why a Typical White Household Has 16 Times the Wealth of a Black One."

11. Sullivan, Meschede, Dietrich, Shapiro, "The Racial Wealth Gap."

CHAPTER 6. THE GENDER WEALTH GAP

1. "Age and Sex Composition: 2010." *Census*. United States Census Bureau, May 2011. Web. 8 Feb. 2018.

2. Faith Guvenen, Greg Kaplan, and Jae Song. "The Glass Ceiling and the Paper Floor: Gender Differences among Top Earners, 1981–2012." *NBER*. National Bureau of Economic Research, Oct. 2014. Web. 8 Feb. 2018.

3. Guvenen, Kaplan, Song, "The Glass Ceiling and the Paper Floor."

4. "Gender Pay Inequality: Consequences for Women, Families, and the Economy." *JEC*. United States Congress Joint Economic Committee, Apr. 2016. Web. 8 Feb. 2018.

5. "Gender Pay Inequality: Consequences for Women, Families, and the Economy."

6. "Gender Pay Inequality: Consequences for Women, Families, and the Economy."

7. Catherine Dunn. "The 1 Percent: How Men and Women Compare in the Top Income Brackets." *IB Times*. Newsweek Media Group, 6 Oct. 2014. Web. 8 Feb. 2018.

8. "Gender Pay Inequality: Consequences for Women, Families, and the Economy."

9. Dunn, "The 1 Percent: How Men and Women Compare in the Top Income Brackets."

10. Guvenen, Kaplan, Song, "The Glass Ceiling and the Paper Floor."

11. "Gender Pay Inequality: Consequences for Women, Families, and the Economy."

12. "Gender Pay Inequality: Consequences for Women, Families, and the Economy."

13. "Gender Pay Inequality: Consequences for Women, Families, and the Economy."

14. Mariko Chang. "Women and Wealth." *Mariko-Chang*. Dallas Women's Foundation, n.d. Web. 8 Feb. 2018.

15. Jennifer Barrett. "What's Worse Than the Gender Wage Gap? The Wealth Gap." *CNBC*. CNBC, 3 Sept. 2015. Web. 8 Feb. 2018.

16. "Gender Pay Inequality: Consequences for Women, Families, and the Economy."

17. "Gender Pay Inequality: Consequences for Women, Families, and the Economy."

CHAPTER 7. WHAT SHOULD BE DONE?

1. "Public Sees Role for Government in Reducing Wealth Inequality." *Washington Post*. Washington Post, 18 Dec. 2013. Web. 8 Feb. 2018.

2. "Public Sees Role for Government in Reducing Wealth Inequality."

3. Christina Pazzanese. "The Costs of Inequality: Increasingly, It's the Rich and the Rest." *Harvard Gazette*. Harvard University, 8 Feb. 2016. Web. 8 Feb. 2018.

4. Michael A. Fletcher and Peyton M. Craighill. "Majority of Americans Want Minimum Wage to Be Increased, Poll Finds." *Washington Post*. Washington Post, 18 Dec. 2013. Web. 8 Feb. 2018.

5. Michael Tanner. "Five Myths about Economic Inequality in America." *CATO*. Cato Institute, 7 Sept. 2016. Web. 8 Feb. 2018.

6. Tanner, "Five Myths about Economic Inequality in America."

7. Tanner, "Five Myths about Economic Inequality in America."

8. John A. Powell. "Economic Inequality: A Defining Issue for America's Future." *Haas Institute*. University of California, Berkeley, 10 Sept. 2014. Web. 8 Feb. 2018.

9. Holly J. Lawrence. "How to Close America's Wealth Gap." *Forbes*. Forbes, 5 Oct. 2016. Web. 8 Feb. 2018.

10. "Just 8 Men Own Same Wealth as Half the World." *Oxfam*. Oxfam International, 16 Jan. 2017. Web. 8 Feb. 2018.

11. "Just 8 Men Own Same Wealth as Half the World."

12. "Just 8 Men Own Same Wealth as Half the World."

13. Stuart M. Butler. "How to Improve Education for Low-Income Students." *Brookings*. Brookings Institution, 5 Jan. 2016. Web. 8 Feb. 2018.

14. John Divine. "How to Solve Income Inequality." *US News*. US News & World Report, 14 Feb. 2017. Web. 8 Feb. 2018.

CHAPTER 8. THE FUTURE OF THE ONE PERCENT

1. Joseph Hines. "Rise in Inequality Projected to Continue until 2035." *Demos*. Demos, 4 June 2013. Web. 8 Feb. 2018.

2. Larry Checco. "The Inequality of the Future?" *Inequality*. Institute for Policy Studies, 5 Nov. 2015. Web. 8 Feb. 2018.

3. Leila Bengali and Mary Daly. "Research, Economic Research, Absolute Mobility, Relative Mobility, American Dream, Economic Mobility." *FRBSF*. Federal Reserve Bank of San Francisco, 4 Mar. 2013. Web. 8 Feb. 2018.

4. Checco, "The Inequality of the Future?"

5. Lauren Gensler. "Rising Income Inequality Is Throwing the Future of Capitalism into Question, Says World Economic Forum." *Forbes*. Forbes, 11 Jan. 2017. Web. 8 Feb. 2018.

6. Michael Tanner. "Five Myths about Economic Inequality in America." *CATO*. Cato Institute, 7 Sept. 2016. Web. 8 Feb. 2018.

7. Matt McFarland. "Robots: Is Your Job at Risk?" *CNN*. Cable News Network, 15 Sept. 2017. Web. 8 Feb. 2018.

8. Bryan Lufkin. "There's a Problem with the Way We Define Inequality." *BBC*. BBC, 7 July 2017. Web. 8 Feb. 2018.

9. Abby Jackson. "Robots Might Be Coming for Our Jobs—But Millennials Aren't Worried." *Business Insider*. Business Insider, 28 Aug. 2017. Web. 8 Feb. 2018.

10. Lufkin, "There's a Problem with the Way We Define Inequality."

INDEX

ABOUT THE
AUTHORS

DUCHESS HARRIS, JD, PHD

Professor Harris is the chair of the American Studies department at Macalester College and curator of the Duchess Harris Collection of ABDO books. She is the author and coauthor of recently released ABDO books including *Hidden Human Computers: The Black Women of NASA*, *Black Lives Matter*, and *Race and Policing*.

Before working with ABDO, she authored several other books on the topics of race, culture, and American history. She served as an associate editor for *Litigation News*, the American Bar Association Section of Litigation's quarterly flagship publication, and was the first editor in chief of *Law Raza*, an interactive online journal covering race and the law, published at William Mitchell College of Law. She has earned a PhD in American Studies from the University of Minnesota and a JD from William Mitchell College of Law.

CARLA MOONEY

Carla Mooney is a graduate of the University of Pennsylvania. Today, she writes for young people and is the author of many books for young adults and children. Mooney enjoys learning about social issues and making the world a more inclusive place for all people.